CAKE

Favourite Foods

Cake
Chips
Chocolate
Ice-Cream
Milkshake
Pizza

All words that appear in **bold** are explained in the glossary on page 30

First published in 1993 by
Wayland (Publishers) Ltd
61 Western Road, Hove
East Sussex BN3 1JD, England
© Copyright 1993 Wayland (Publishers) Ltd

Editor: Francesca Motisi
Research: Anne Moses

British Library Cataloguing in Publication Data
Moses, Brian
    Cake.—(Favourite Foods Series)
    I. Title II. Gordon, Mike III. Series
    664

    ISBN 0-7502-0633-0

Typeset by Dorchester Typesetting Group Ltd
Printed and bound in Belgium by Casterman, S.A.

CAKE

Written by Brian Moses

Illustrated by Mike Gordon

Wayland

When did you last tuck
into a cream cake?

Or maybe you prefer
sinking your teeth
into a slice of sponge.

Perhaps you'd rather nibble
a piece of fruit cake.

Or feast your eyes
on a chocolate
surprise!

To make a cake you need some flour,

margarine or butter,

sugar and eggs.

Many types of cake can be made by adding other **ingredients**.

The ingredients are mixed together and rise when the cake is baked in an oven.

Currants, raisins and sultanas are
often used to make rich fruit cakes.
These dried fruits come from countries
such as Africa and the West Indies.

They were first brought back to Britain by sailors and **explorers** almost five hundred years ago.

Long ago, cakes were only cooked and eaten on special occasions. They used to be sweetened with honey.

Sugar, butter and eggs were very expensive until **Victorian** times. Bakers then began to sell ready-made cakes.

We can make cakes at home,
or buy them from a bakery,
or a supermarket.

The cakes in the supermarket are made in factories like this one.

In a British teashop you can eat **scones** with jam and cream, followed by cake!

In the USA you can eat all sorts of cakes including chocolate brownies and carrot cake.

Germany is famous for its chocolate
cake filled with cream and cherries.
It is called Black Forest Gateau,
after the area it comes from.

In New Zealand and Australia, a large **meringue** cake covered with whipped cream and fruit is called a 'pavlova'. It is named after the ballet dancer Anna Pavlova.

Many cakes are baked for special occasions. Birthday cakes are usually iced. Candles are placed on the cake, one for each year of the child's life.

In some countries wedding cakes can have two or three **tiers**. These are iced and decorated with good luck charms such as horseshoes.

Simnel cakes are baked at Easter time. These are rich fruit cakes, topped with a layer of **marzipan**.

Chocolate cakes in the shape of a **Yule log** are often eaten at Christmas time.

Swimming Pool Cake

This is a recipe for a fun cake that you can make yourself. You will need a little help from an adult when it comes to using the oven and cutting out icing.

For the cake itself you will need:

2 packets (2×225g) sponge cake mix
An 18×23×4cm (7×9×1½ inches)
cake tin

For the icing you will need:

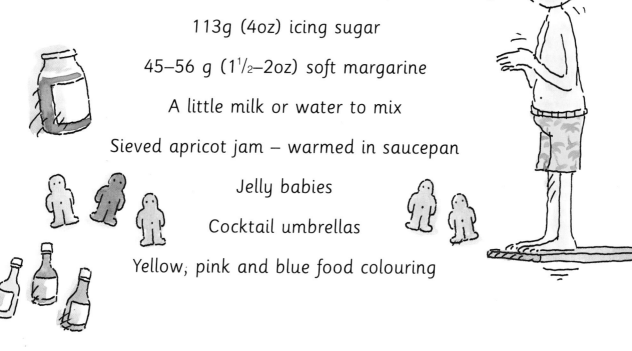

Approx. 285g (10oz) 'ready-to-roll' soft white icing

113g (4oz) icing sugar

45–56 g (1½–2oz) soft margarine

A little milk or water to mix

Sieved apricot jam – warmed in saucepan

Jelly babies

Cocktail umbrellas

Yellow, pink and blue food colouring

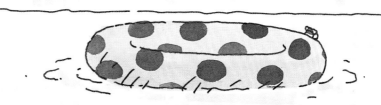

This is what you do:

1   Ask an adult to help you make this recipe. Follow directions on the sponge cake packets. Bake large cake for about 25 minutes, then cool before icing.

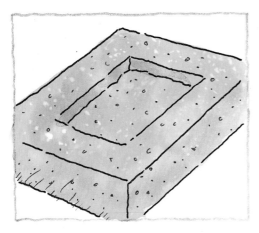

2   Mark a smaller rectangle (11 × 15 cm approx.) in the middle of the cake and scoop a little of the cake off the top. This is for the water in the swimming pool.

3   Roll out soft white icing to rectangular shape.

4 Using a rolling pin and knife, cut strips of white icing. Spread a little apricot jam over sides and top edges of pool. Fit strips on these areas. See diagram.

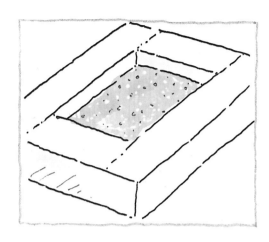

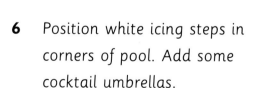

5 Make some balls and small towels by mixing a little colouring with soft white icing and squeezing or pressing into shape.

6 Position white icing steps in corners of pool. Add some cocktail umbrellas.

 7 Beat together icing sugar, butter or soft margarine and a little water to make butter icing.

8 Add the blue food colouring and cover scooped-out area of swimming pool. Make surface ripples with a fork.

 9 Position jelly babies on towels using spots of icing. Put others in the pool and around the edges. Some can have icing armbands.

10 Now arrange balls, umbrellas and small towels around
the swimming pool.

What other shapes can you think of for cakes?

Cakes

Our baker bakes such lovely cakes
and puts them on display.
I sometimes think that I could stand
and stare at them all day.

There are sponge cakes of all shape and sizes,
iced fancies and chocolate whirls,
giant Swiss rolls and creamy puffs,
Danish pastries and coconut twirls.

There's one that's shaped like the Eiffel Tower
and some wonderful wedding cakes.
But nothing in our baker's window
matches the ones that my Mum makes…

(and she's baking me one for my tea!)

Glossary

Explorers   People who travel to a country and find out about it.

Ingredients   All the different things needed to make something e.g. a cake.

Marzipan   A mixture of almonds, sugar and egg that is used on top of cakes.

Meringue   A crisp cake that is made from sugar mixed with the whites of eggs and then baked.

Scones   Small plain cakes made with flour and very little fat, usually served split open and buttered.

Tiers   Several layers that are placed on top of each other.

Victorian   Something that happened during the reign of Queen Victoria, 1837-1901.

Yule log   Yule is an old-fashioned word for Christmas. The yule log was used to start an open fire at Christmas. This was before the days of electricity and central heating, so the tradition has almost died out now.

Acknowledgements
The author and publisher would like to thank the Biscuits, Cakes, Chocolate and Confectionery Alliance for their advice.

Notes for parents and teachers

Read the book with children, either individually or in groups. Ask for comments about the illustrations as you turn each page. Which cakes do children like best? Write about them and draw pictures.

Suggest that children bring to school empty cake boxes. Talk about the ingredients. How much do the cakes cost and how many are there in each box? Which ones are the best value for money?

Part of the classroom might become a baker's shop. Children could write out price lists and make up shopping bills to swap with each other.

Read some of the stories mentioned in 'Books to read'. Ask the children to write their own stories about making unusual cakes, or about the trouble that is caused when someone tries to bake a cake.

Children may enjoy inventing a new type of cake. What will it be called and what will it look like? Ask them to list the ingredients and design an advertisement with an eye-catching slogan. Suggest that children then write out recipes for a witch's cake, a dragon's cake, a giant's cake, etc.

What other information can children discover about cakes from different countries? Discuss how this information might be gathered. Could the findings be displayed around a large map of the world?

Children who attempt the recipe for a 'Swimming Pool Cake' will be finding similarities and differences in a variety of cooking materials. They will discover how food changes when different ingredients are mixed together i.e. icing sugar and soft margarine with a little water, and how the sponge mix changes when it is cooked.

Children should be able to talk about what they have done and to be able to put into order the different steps in the making of their cake.

The above suggestions will satisfy a number of statements of attainment in National Curriculum guidelines for English, Maths and Science at Key Stage 1.

Books to read

A Packet of Poems – Poems about food, selected by
Jill Bennett (OUP, 1982).

A Picnic of Poetry – Poems about food and drink,
selected by Anne Harvey (Blackie 1988/Puffin 1990).

Quick, Let's Get Out of Here – by Michael Rosen
(Puffin, 1985) includes the poem Chocolate Cake – a
real gem for reading aloud.

The Cake That Mack Ate by Rose Robart/Maryann
Kovalski (Picture Puffin, 1990).

The Doorbell Rang by Pat Hutchins (Picture Puffin,
1988).

Maurice's Mum by Roger Smith (Picture Puffin, 1991).

The Witch in the Cherry Tree by Margaret Mahy
(Picture Puffin, 1987).

Index